GREENWICH
THEN & NOW
IN COLOUR

BARBARA LUDLOW & JULIAN WATSON

First published in 2012

The History Press
The Mill, Brimscombe Port
Stroud, Gloucestershire, GL5 2QG
www.thehistorypress.co.uk

ISBN 978 0 7524 6875 4

Typesetting and origination by The History Press
Printed in India.
Manufacturing managed by Jellyfish Print Solutions Ltd

CONTENTS

ACKNOWLEDGEMENTS

This book would not have been possible without the unstinting support and help of the staff of the Greenwich Heritage Centre at Woolwich. Their expertise and endless patience is much appreciated.

With the exception of one photograph, all the old photographs and postcards used in this book are from the very large and impressive collections at the Heritage Centre. Many of the photographs taken in the 1930s are by Alan Roger Martin, the Blackheath antiquarian, whose collections are housed there. His photographs are a unique and fascinating record of the Greenwich district before the devastation of the Second World War and the changes brought about by post-war redevelopment.

We would like to thank: Neil Rhind MBE, FSA for permission to use the picture of the Folly Pond on Blackheath; Peter Guillery for detailed information about buildings in Woolwich; Darrell Spurgeon, whose *Discover* series of architectural guides have been invaluable and who is quoted in the text; and Chris Harrison for permission to use his photograph from the top of Cox's Mount in Maryon Park, Charlton.

ABOUT THE AUTHORS

Julian Watson is a retired chartered librarian who was head of the Local History and Archives Service for the London Borough of Greenwich from 1969 until his retirement in 2003. Julian and Barbara Ludlow worked together as colleagues for many years at Greenwich Local History Library in Blackheath. He is now hon. editor and vice president of the Greenwich Historical Society. He researches, writes and lectures on Greenwich history. He has written and co-written five books on Greenwich, and contributed many articles to the *Journal of the Greenwich Historical Society* and its predecessor, the *Journal of the Greenwich and Lewisham Antiquarian Society*. He served as president and vice president of the Antiquarian Society. He has also written a series of historical articles for the *News Shopper* newspaper. In addition, he co-edited a book on the history of the Royal Arsenal at Woolwich. He is a former churchwarden of St Mary's church, Lewisham, and published a history of it in 2004.

Barbara Ludlow was born in Greenwich and lived there until, in retirement, she moved to Kent. She studied at the University of London for a Diploma in Local History and became a local studies lecturer at Greenwich Adult Education Institute. She later served as Education Officer at Greenwich Local History Library, where she worked with Julian Watson. She continued her career as a local studies lecturer after her retirement from the library. She has written three books on Greenwich, co-written four others and contributed articles on local history to: *Bygone Kent* magazine, the *South East London Mercury* newspaper, the *Transactions of the Greenwich and Lewisham Antiquarian Society* and the *Journal of the Greenwich Historical Society*. Barbara, like Julian, served as president and vice president of the Antiquarian Society and is vice president of the Greenwich Historical Society.

INTRODUCTION

The year 2012 is an exciting time for the Borough of Greenwich. Most importantly, it will become a Royal Borough. The Olympic and Paralympic equestrian events will be hosted in Greenwich Park and shooting events at the Royal Artillery barracks in Woolwich. In addition, a cable-car connection between the O2 at Greenwich and the north bank of the Thames is proposed. Many regeneration and improvement projects are under way or will be completed: the landscaping of Cutty Sark gardens, the new Greenwich Pier, the redevelopment of the Ferrier Estate in Kidbrooke, continuing development on the historic Royal Arsenal site at Woolwich and on the Greenwich Peninsula. The theme of transition and change, ever present in the Borough's history, is as powerful now as it has ever been.

The photographs in this book were taken, and the text written, before many of these events and during construction of the projects listed above, so readers must excuse what may appear to be omissions or images that do not reflect the scale of change. Some viewpoints, for instance, were difficult or impossible to access. However, we hope that many of the great changes from the nineteenth- and twentieth-century photographs will be very apparent. This is a 'then and now' tour of the Royal Borough of Greenwich using historical photographs selected, almost entirely, from the Greenwich Heritage Centre. All the modern photographs save one were taken by Julian Watson.

Before the end of the last century, many of Greenwich's traditional industries, which had given work to local people – shipbuilding, barge building, the manufacture of armaments – had disappeared. The closure of the East Greenwich Gas Works, for example, left the northern portion of the Greenwich Peninsula, formerly called 'The Marsh', virtually derelict. After negotiations between the government and the site owners, much of this old gas-works site was used for building the Millennium Dome, which was ready by New Year's Eve 1999. It is now, as the O$_2$ Arena, one of the world's most important and successful venues for the arts, music and sporting events, and of course has been nominated as an Olympic venue for the 2012 London games.

Woolwich has also been affected by major changes over the centuries; in 1869 the Woolwich Royal Dockyard closed overnight and many of the Dockyard's workforce took up the Government's offer to emigrate with their families and resettle in Canada. This closure was the beginning of the end of state employment in Woolwich. In 1967 the Royal Ordnance Factories in the Arsenal were closed. This old and huge industrial complex stretched from Woolwich, across the Plumstead Marshes, and was known as a 'town within a town'.

Woolwich was first and foremost a military town and features on the Army's list of garrison towns. The Royal Regiment of Artillery has now gone but their magnificent barracks still accommodate companies of soldiers. However, the Royal Military Academy and the Royal Herbert Hospital are no longer in military use: they have been converted for housing.

The re-development of the docks on the northern side of the Thames affected both Greenwich and Woolwich; the Royal Docks in North Woolwich is now the location of The London City Airport. Empty industrial sites in Greenwich have been cleared and re-developed as expensive housing complexes. Clearly it has become very fashionable to live by the Thames where once noxious industries proliferated. Indeed, many new estates have been built, part of the dramatic changes witnessed by the now Royal Borough of Greenwich and its inhabitants over the centuries.

ROYAL GREENWICH

THE TOP PHOTOGRAPH here was taken from a high point either on or above Observatory Hill, Greenwich Park in 1879. Greenwich Park, the oldest of the royal parks, was formed by Humphrey, Duke of Gloucester, when he enclosed ground on Blackheath and in Greenwich in 1433. He attached this new park to a house on the riverside, which he acquired after the death of Thomas Beaufort. Later, in 1675, the Royal Observatory was built on the site of Duke Humphrey's Tower: a small fortress or watchtower built on the high ground of what is now Observatory Hill. After his death in 1447, his house and land in Greenwich reverted to the Crown and his house, Bella Court, became the home of Margaret of Anjou. The house was much improved and renamed Placentia.

It was eventually demolished and rebuilt by Henry VII as Greenwich Palace. This splendid Tudor palace on the riverside became the birthplace of Henry VIII, Mary Tudor and Elizabeth I. A gatehouse straddled the main road from London to North Kent, connecting park and palace. It is recorded that Elizabeth I sat in the gatehouse to view military parades in the park. When the Stuarts arrived in Greenwich Henry VIII's buildings were felt to be out-of-date, so Inigo Jones was commissioned to design a house in the Palladian style for Anne of Denmark, wife of James I. This prestigious building was also built across the busy main road. The Queen's House can be seen right of centre in this photograph.

During the Civil War and afterwards, the old palace crumbled. John Webb designed a new palace for Charles II which would allow the Queen's House to have an unbroken view to the Thames. Only one building, with the inscription *Carolus Rex*, was finished before the money ran out.

William and Mary did not want to live in Greenwich and, in 1694, Queen Mary decreed that

the site be used for a Royal Hospital for Seamen, the naval equivalent of the Chelsea Hospital. The architect of the Royal Hospital for Seamen was Christopher Wren. The Greenwich Pensioners left in 1869 and the buildings became the Royal Naval College in 1873. In 1806 the Queen's House became part of the Royal Naval Asylum School and the wings and colonnades were built. In the 1820s the whole complex became the Greenwich Hospital Schools until the school moved to Holbrook in Suffolk in 1933.

THE INCOMPARABLE VICTORIAN panorama seems to have been taken from a greater height than was possible for the modern view. The modern version from the General Wolfe Statue cannot show us the marvellous detail of West Greenwich revealed in the 1879 image, but it does show much of the World Heritage Site. The Queen's House is the centre block of the National Maritime Museum and the Old Royal Naval College, which now houses the University of Greenwich and Trinity College of Music. On the Greenwich Peninsula, the O_2, formerly the Millennium Dome, and modern housing developments have replaced most of the heavy industries and also the huge East Greenwich Gas Works, once the largest in the world. Greenwich Park hosts the Olympic equestrian events this year (2012); the presence of so many galloping horses will be reminiscent of the park in its Tudor heyday.

7

THE *CUTTY SARK* AND CUTTY SARK GARDENS

THE SHIP HOTEL and Garden Stairs (opposite). Alan Roger Martin's atmospheric photograph, taken in 1937, is of the Ship Hotel before it was destroyed in the Second World War. Two men and a girl stand on Garden Stairs looking across to Johnson's Drawdock on the Isle of Dogs, where H. Clark and Sons are advertising 'Anti-fouling Compositions for Ships' Bottoms.'

Alongside the stairs is the famous Ship Hotel. Many people wined and dined at this fashionable venue, designed by Philip Hardwick and built 1853-1858. It was much larger then: part of the building and the large snooker hall were demolished in 1908 and thirteen houses built on the site. The design of the Ship had to accommodate an old right of way: the last remnant of Fisher Lane, an ancient street that once ran through the town as far as the Royal Naval College. This lane was part of a network of alleys, lanes and courts which covered the riverside area, including what is now Cutty Sark Gardens. Before these buildings – part of the ancient town centre of Greenwich – were demolished, it was only possible to get occasional glimpses of the Thames; today we can enjoy fine, unobstructed river views. The Ship Hotel was bombed in 1941 and the site was cleared in the 1950s to make a dock for the *Cutty Sark* clipper ship. The adjacent Dodd's Wharf was also cleared to make Cutty Sark Gardens.

CUTTY SARK GARDENS, the *Cutty Sark* and the Greenwich Foot Tunnel (above). Taking photographs here was difficult, with scaffolding and hoardings surrounding this ancient riverside site, so, instead of the usual 'now' photograph, this is a view of the whole site from the top floor of the Meridian estate. A kind resident gave us access to his flat. The *Cutty Sark* clipper is emerging from its protective covering as the restoration work following the terrible fire of 2007 nears completion. Cutty Sark Gardens, an open space created from an important and once densely occupied riverside area, is being re-landscaped as a more attractive setting for the restored *Cutty Sark* clipper in its dry dock. The Greenwich Foot Tunnel of 1902 is being refurbished as well. Garden Stairs, the ancient entry into the town from the river, is still there next to the Foot Tunnel. The domes of the William and Mary blocks of the Old Royal Naval College can be seen above the trees.

THE *FAME* AND THE OLD ROYAL NAVAL COLLEGE

A 1920S VIEW (right) of the *Fame* training ship on the forecourt of the Queen's House. Boys in their thousands passed through the Greenwich Hospital School in the nineteenth and early twentieth centuries. This mock ship, one of several, was built as a training ship for the boys. When the school moved to Suffolk in 1933, the ship was demolished. The vacant school buildings and the Queen's House became the National Maritime Museum, which was opened by George VI in 1937.

NO TRACE OF the *Fame* now remains – just a beautiful lawn leading down to Romney Road and the Queen Mary block of the Old Royal Naval College, now part of the University of Greenwich. The chapel, originally the chapel of the former Royal Hospital for Seamen, is in this building. Designed by James Stuart and opened in 1789, it replaced the original chapel, which had been destroyed by fire.

THE DREADNOUGHT SEAMEN'S HOSPITAL, ROMNEY ROAD

THIS BUILDING WAS opened in 1764 as the infirmary for pensioners in the Royal Hospital for Seamen, later the Royal Naval College. In 1870, after the closure of the Royal Hospital, the Seamen's Hospital Society took a lease of the building, enabling it to move its hospital from

the *Dreadnought* on the Thames to this much more appropriate site. The Hospital for Tropical Diseases in Euston grew out of the expertise and experience gained in the *Dreadnought* hulk at Greenwich, where sailors suffering from diseases contracted in many parts of the world were treated.

THE DREADNOUGHT SEAMEN'S Hospital closed in 1986 and the building's future was uncertain. After restoration in 1998-9 by Dannatt, Johnson and Partners, it was opened as the Dreadnought Library and Learning Centre, part of the University of Greenwich.

BILLINGSGATE DOCK

IN THE PHOTOGRAPH on the right by A.R.
Martin, children stand where the fishing
smacks were tied up in the nineteenth century.
Billingsgate Dock and Ship Dock to the east were
the two most important docks in Greenwich.
The weatherboard building belonged to D. and E.
Noakes, forage merchants and inventors of the
'Noakesoscope', a multiple-lens magic-lantern
projector.

THERE HAS BEEN little change to Billingsgate
Dock itself, but its setting has changed.
Noakes' building has gone, as have many of
the old riverside streets like Billingsgate Street,
Brewhouse lane and the grimly named Dark

Entry. Some streets went with the building of the Meridian estate, one block of which can be seen in this picture; others were finally cleared for the laying out of Cutty Sark Gardens.

GREENWICH PIER

IN 1935, AN Eagle Pleasure Steamer waits at Greenwich Pier to take Londoners on a trip
to Margate or Ramsgate. The Eagle ships were part of the dramatic rescue of British troops
from the beaches of Dunkirk in 1940. The *Crested Eagle* was sunk. Beside the pier, facing the
camera, once stood Ship Dock, the principal dock of the town.

GREENWICH PIER IS being rebuilt. A day trip to Greenwich by boat is still the most popular
option for tourists, as it has been since the pier opened in 1836. Tourists crowd the streets

and the historic buildings during the summer – and even the winter. Similar numbers flocked to the town at Bank Holidays in the nineteenth century to enjoy the very rowdy Greenwich Fair, which was closed in 1857.

GREENWICH BEACH

THE LOW TIDE beach at Greenwich has always been an attraction and often a substitute for
a seaside holiday. It had its dangers: polluted water and very powerful tides. But many people
enjoyed this beach and learned to swim there. The Medical Officer of Health for Greenwich in
1900 expressed grave concern about illnesses that children suffered after holidaying on the beach.
Nevertheless, at the beginning of the 1930s, George Lansbury, Commissioner of Works in the

Labour Government, set out to provide open-air amenities for children in the poorer districts of London. At certain places on the Thames, sand from seaside resorts such as Margate was deposited on the foreshore to enhance the low-tide beach. This area of beach was always much enjoyed. Spritsail barges, the workhorses of the Thames, are seen moored here.

TODAY GREENWICH IS not the seaside resort that it was when the postcard view was taken but its beach is still a place to enjoy when the sun is shining and the river is calm. There are much fewer craft on the Thames now, of course, and the river is very much cleaner.

19

GREENWICH CHURCH STREET

GREENWICH CHURCH STREET, *c.* 1890
(right). The railway line connecting
Greenwich Station to Maze Hill was
constructed in 1878. Next to the London &
County Bank (first right), the South Eastern
railway is advertising 'Land to be Let'.
The tram routes linking Greenwich with
Westminster and Blackfriars started in 1871.
Greenwich Church Street was full of shops.
Henry Richardson's bookshop is next to the
bank and, on the far corner of Nelson Road
and Church Street, Leverett & Frye's large
grocery store can be seen. The entrance to
Turnpin Lane is quite clear. A few shops
further down, Mr Bartle, the dentist, has

an advert above a chemist's shop. The west end of St Alfege church is on the left of the photograph and opposite the bank.

GREENWICH CHURCH STREET, the ancient high street leading to Garden Stairs on the Thames, is difficult to photograph at the moment because of modern street furniture and parked vehicles. The east end of St Alfege church is about to be cleaned, hence the hoarding. It will then match the splendour of the newly cleaned west end. The church is a dominant feature of this important street. The many modern intrusions have made it impossible to match the splendid Victorian photograph.

ST ALFEGE CHURCH

THE PARISH CHURCH of Greenwich, featured in the Victorian photograph on the right, was built to the designs of Nicholas Hawksmoor in 1711-14, and the spire was added by John James in 1730. The nave of an earlier church, said to have been built on the spot where Archbishop Alfege was murdered by the Danes in 1012, collapsed during a storm in 1710. The ancient church became the royal church when the Tudors held court in Greenwich Palace. Thomas Tallis was the royal organist from 1540 to 1585, and a sixteenth-century organ console, thought to have been used by him, is on show behind glass in the nave of the church. The interior of the church was

badly damaged by incendiaries during the Second World War. Most of Grinling Gibbon's carvings and much else was destroyed when the roof was set on fire and crashed into the church, bringing down its great oval ceiling.

THE MODERN PHOTOGRAPH of St Alfege church on the left is interrupted by a piece of modern technology: a solar-powered traffic sign.

ST MARY'S CHURCH, KING WILLIAM WALK

THE ARCHITECT OF this church was George Basevi, a cousin of Benjamin Disraeli. St Mary's was built as the daughter church of St Alfege to cope with a burgeoning congregation. Paradoxically, however, by 1919 the congregation had dwindled and, in 1936, the decision to demolish it was taken. A photographer captured the beginning of its destruction from a viewpoint in Nevada Street. Two men are standing on the roof quite unprotected but a man close by seems unperturbed.

IT SEEMS INCREDIBLE that such an imposing church could have gone and radically changed the view along Nevada Street. Stones marked the site of the church and a statue of William IV by Samuel Nixon was moved to this spot from King William Street in the City of London in 1936. The statue now stands in the newly landscaped grounds of the Sammy Ofer Wing of the National Maritime Museum. This new wing was opened in July 2011.

GREENWICH'S FIRST TOWN HALL

THE PHOTOGRAPH BELOW, from around 1925, is of an impressive building which was erected in 1876 for the use of the Greenwich District Board of Works. When Greenwich

became a Metropolitan Borough in 1900 it was used as the Town Hall. A new Town Hall, further along Greenwich High Road, was built in 1939. The former building became a council community centre.

A DRAMATICALLY DIFFERENT scene is there today. The former Town Hall was badly damaged in the Second World War and lost its impressive dome. It is now Greenwich West Community Centre. The fine adjoining terrace, Vansittart Terrace, was completely destroyed, and tyres and exhausts are now fitted on that site.

GREENWICH HIGH ROAD

THE PHOTOGRAPH ON the left shows the junction of Greenwich High Road and Greenwich South Street – one of a series of photographs of 1885 commissioned by the Revd Charles Spurgeon, a Baptist minister in Greenwich. The hay cart may have come from the rural areas of Kidbrooke or Eltham. Water for the horses was from troughs supplied by the Metropolitan Drinking Fountain and Cattle Trough Association. The lamp on the drinking fountain was left to the people of Greenwich by Sir David Salomons, a former Member of Parliament for Greenwich. In 1888 the right-hand side of Duncan's Pharmacy was a bakery and a post office. The left-hand side was an upholsterer's shop.

THE MODERN PHOTOGRAPH above, taken from a similar viewpoint, opposite Prince of Orange Lane, is in stark contrast to the photograph of 1885: the road is unusually quiet, with not a car in sight! The house on the right-hand side of Prince of Orange Lane is the beginning of Bexley Place – an elegant group of buildings, constructed in around 1815. The interesting street furniture of 1885 didn't survive the transition from horse transport to the age of cars, lorries and buses.

A GREENWICH BREWERY, GREENWICH HIGH ROAD

JOHN LOVIBOND FOUNDED the Nag's Head Brewery in Greenwich in 1826. The brewery moved to premises in Greenwich High Road in 1865. The 1930s photograph on the right is by A.R. Martin. As well as acquiring other breweries, they also ran public houses, hotels and off-licences in the south of England. Lovibond's Greenwich Brewery closed in 1962. E.W. (Billy) Briselden was the last Master Brewer at Lovibond's.

FROM BREWING TO consuming and retailing: Davy's Wine Bar took over the Lovibond buildings and the wine vaults are at the heart of Greenwich's old brewery. Brewing has not gone from Greenwich: Alastair Hook, Brewmaster, set up the renowned Meantime Brewery in 2000.

GREENWICH HIGH ROAD
AND ITS SHOPS

PHOTOGRAPHED IN 1937 by A.R. Martin, the shop fronts in the picture opposite, in what was still London Street, are built on the front gardens of eighteenth- and nineteenth-century houses. In 1924, Munyard's store advertised its home-killed meat, cooked meats, grocery and provisions, wines, spirits and bottled beers. Next door was Streak's the fishmonger, and the whole became a general store. Munyard also had shops in East Greenwich and Blackheath.

STREAK AND MUNYARD'S shops, originally numbered 46-50 London Street, stood in front of what is now this small modern precinct in Greenwich High Road. The precinct was set back from the road to provide parking for shoppers, something that was not needed when the old shops were there. This important shopping street was badly damaged in the Second World War but shops are still an important feature.

BATHS AND WASH-HOUSES

THE HIGHLY DECORATIVE building seen in the photograph on the right opened in 1851 and was thought to be an extravagance by some ratepayers. However, the *Greenwich Mercury* in July 1853 stated that the 'present weather is a powerful advocate in favour of baths and wash-houses.' These baths and wash-houses were closed in 1928 when new swimming baths (now the Arches Leisure Centre) were opened in East Greenwich.

THE BUILDINGS ON this site included not only the old baths and wash-houses but also Morton's Theatre, where Edgar Wallace's mother Polly Richards acted. All the buildings were demolished to make way for the Metropolitan Borough of Greenwich's fine new Town Hall, designed by Clifford Culpin and opened in 1939. Following the

formation of the London Borough of Greenwich in 1965, the Town Hall staff were transferred to Woolwich and this building was sold. The Greenwich School of Management now occupies Meridian House, but Greenwich Council retains the Borough Hall round the corner in Royal Hill.

ANTIQUES AND ENTERTAINMENT

IN THE 1970s, tourists and locals visited this open-air antiques market. The early 1970s photograph on the right records the arrival of a coach full of tourists. The police had put down 'no parking' cones so that through traffic wouldn't be obstructed. A stall selling Victorian dresses was very popular. In the background, towering above the stalls, is John Humphries' House, built in 1963 to house a Leo III computer, which was used by the London Borough's Joint Computer Committee. The Metropolitan Borough of Greenwich was the lead authority in this innovative, cost-sharing venture whereby the six boroughs shared this huge computer to carry out a wide range of financial and other tasks. John Humphries was Greenwich's Borough Treasurer.

THE GREENWICH PICTUREHOUSE is a fine modern multi-screen cinema in Greenwich High Road (formerly London Street). Trees mask John Humphries' House in Stockwell Street in the modern photograph on the right. This pioneering computer services building was demolished at the end of 2011 to make way for the new University of Greenwich School of Architecture buildings. Greenwich Clock Tower antiques and craft market operates in the open area at weekends.

CRANE STREET
AND HIGHBRIDGE

A PHOTOGRAPH BY A.R. Martin of the riverside at Crane Street and Highbridge in 1938. From right to left, we have: the Trafalgar Tavern, built in 1837; the Yacht Tavern; Corbett and Son, boat builders; and Greenwich Power Station, supplying electricity for London's trams. Trinity Hospital, an almshouse founded in 1614, next to the power station, is hidden from sight.

NO BOATS IN this scene, but the members of the rowing clubs can be regularly seen sculling on the river and then taking their boats up the beach and through the draw dock at the end of Crane Street. The scene is very similar except for the new riverside houses on Highbridge. The power-station coaling pier is still there but no longer used. Crane Street, behind the Trafalgar and Yacht Taverns, is a narrow, attractive and ancient riverside alley, which has survived many periods of re-development and change. It leads to Highbridge, once home to Tudor courtiers, where the massive bulk of the power station dwarfs the small and attractive Trinity Hospital Almshouses.

BALLAST QUAY, EAST GREENWICH

ON THE EXTREME right of the old photograph of Ballast Quay is the Union Tavern (now the Cutty Sark Tavern). A.R. Martin took the photograph in 1937. Richard Hannam was the publican of this picturesque riverside public house at the time. In the far distance is the harbourmaster's office, built in 1855 to control collier traffic on the Thames. Ballast Quay was badly damaged in the Second World War but was quickly restored

THE 2009 VIEW above looks similar to the original photograph because of the cranes, but these are not the cranes for unloading cargoes at Lovell's Wharf: they are for the housing development on the wharf. The riverside area here is attractive: the beer garden of the pub is beside the river and the old Harbour Master's Wharf is now a private garden. Change to this area in recent years has been dramatic, particularly with the closure of the long-established scrap-metal yard on Crowley's Wharf to the west of the 1937 photograph but out of view. That yard was the last link with the warehouse of Ambrose Crowley, the greatest Iron Master of his day. He moved to Crowley House on Highbridge in 1704 and built his huge warehouse next to his home. House and warehouse were on the site of the power station to the west of Ballast Quay.

RIVER BANK,
EAST GREENWICH

IN 1937 THE wharves and factories on the west side of the
Blackwall Peninsula were part of Greenwich's industrial
heartland, which developed in the nineteenth century.
The photograph on the right is by A.R. Martin. The many
industries included making submarine cables, barge builders,
a soap and candle factory, stone and cement works, a
pet-food manufactory and a maize refinery. Unlike factories
in northern towns, no one industry was dominant. The
gasholders were part of the East Greenwich Gasworks, the
site of which is now the O_2 Arena.

A VERY DRAMATIC change in East Greenwich: the working
riverside has almost disappeared. Silver birches and shrubs
now line Lovell's Wharf, a landing place where, within
recent memory, freight-carrying craft arrived from Europe
to discharge their cargoes. Now the area is a quiet housing
development with wonderful views up and down the Thames.
The riverside in the background is about to experience
similar changes, with a proposed cruise-liner terminal and
further riverside housing.

THE SEA WITCH
PUBLIC HOUSE

THE PHOTOGRAPH ON the left, taken in 1937 by A.R. Martin, shows the Sea Witch public house and Hollick's Wharf opposite each other on the East Greenwich riverside. The public house was often used as a 'signing-on' office for casual river workers. The Sea Witch and Hollick's Wharf received direct hits during the Blitz in 1940.

THE SEA WITCH pub was demolished and the site taken over by Tunnel Refineries. Now Tunnel Refineries has been demolished and the site awaits redevelopment. The pub stood close to the river behind the trees and adjacent to the warehouse wall. This photograph had to be taken from a Thames Clipper because the whole of this section of the riverside path (2011) is closed.

45

COMBE FARM AND
EAST GREENWICH

COMBE FARM IS recorded in one of the great works of English literature. Samuel Pepys
moved his wife to Woolwich during the 1665 plague and he often walked from Greenwich
along the ancient Woolwich Road to visit her. On 4 September he wrote in his diary: 'It
troubled me to pass by Come Farm where about 21 people have died of the plague – and
three or four days since I saw a dead corpse in a coffin lie in the close unburied…'

The farm was shut up and guarded by the parish watch and subsequently sold to James Hayes,
a city merchant. In 1672 it was licensed as a Congregational Meeting House. Later, in 1795, a
new farmhouse was built. In 1838 John Angerstein of Woodlands purchased Combe Farm and
in 1846 leased it to Mary Roberts, a market gardener. It is the Roberts family and Angerstein's
land agent who are in the remarkable photograph opposite, which was taken in 1858 by
Mr Gay. The spread of suburbia gradually engulfed the fields and, in 1901, the farmhouse
was demolished. The South Eastern Railway arrived close to Combe Farm in the 1870s and
Nathaniel Roberts bought the first railway ticket sold at Westcombe Park Station.

THE MODERN PANORAMA above is a great contrast to the peaceful rural scene of 1858. The
A102 thrusts through the fields and marshlands of Combe Farm on its way to the Blackwall
Tunnel at the northern extremity of the Greenwich Peninsula. The 1858 photograph was taken
around the corner, among the houses on the left-hand side of the modern picture.

'WOODLANDS', MYCENAE ROAD, BLACKHEATH

'WOODLANDS', DESIGNED BY George Gibson in 1774 for John Julius Angerstein, the 'Father of Lloyd's', acquired an extension as the Angerstein family grew. Sir Alfred Yarrow, the shipbuilder, bought the house in 1896. In the photograph on the left he and his family are having tea in the garden. Yarrow moved his shipyard to the Upper Clyde in 1906 but he remained the owner of 'Woodlands' until 1923, when he sold it to the Little Sisters of the Assumption. In 1967 the London Borough of Greenwich bought Woodlands and the adjoining novitiate house. The latter became Kidbrooke House Community Centre (now Mycenae House) and Woodlands became Greenwich Local History Library. The official opening of the Local History Library and Woodlands Art Gallery took place in 1972, although the library had been open there since 1970.

WOODLANDS HAS BEEN beautifully restored and now houses the Greenwich Steiner School. Greenwich Local History Library moved from Woodlands in 2003 to amalgamate with the Greenwich Borough Museum on a new site in the Royal Arsenal, Woolwich. The Greenwich Heritage Centre, the result of the amalgamation, opened in the same year.

BLACKWALL TUNNEL SOUTHERN APPROACH ROAD

IN THE 1960s a second Blackwall Tunnel was under construction. Local roads were unable to cope with the ever-increasing number of vehicles using the original tunnel of 1897 . A new dual carriageway, called the Blackwall Tunnel Southern Approach Road, was commissioned in the late 1960s. Many houses and shops were demolished, but a row of shops and the Sun in the Sands public house were spared. They can be seen in the left-hand corner of the 1968 photograph on the right.

UNUSUALLY LIGHT TRAFFIC on the A102 road from the Blackwall Tunnel. On the left is the slip road to the Sun in the Sands roundabout, named after the pub of that name. Beyond the roundabout the A102 and the A2 merge. The old A2, formerly the Dover Road, the Canterbury Way and Watling Street, made its way in a straight line over Shooters Hill to Welling and, finally, to Dover. In 1968 a group of historians from the Greenwich and Lewisham Antiquarian Society examined what appeared to be a section of Roman road on a chalk foundation in Old Dover Road, close to the viewpoint of this photograph. The section of Roman road was on the same alignment as Old Dover Road and headed towards the Vanbrugh Gate of Greenwich Park.

FOLLY POND AND THE BLACKHEATH GATE TO GREENWICH PARK

IT'S HOLIDAY TIME in the photograph on the left from about 1925, with children paddling and boating on the pond made out of an old gravel pit in the 1890s.

MANY MORE TREES now encircle the much smaller Folly Pond, making it harder to see the Blackheath Gate of Greenwich Park from where thousands of London Marathon runners have poured every April since 1981. Neither is the pond the focus of holidaymakers as it was decades ago, when it was also a boating pond. Apart from the adjacent donkey rides, Folly Pond is largely unnoticed – although it teems with wildlife and adds tranquillity to a part of the Heath next to the busy A2.

CHARLTON HOUSE

SIR ADAM NEWTON, tutor to Prince Henry, the son of James I and brother of Charles I, acquired the Manor of Charlton in 1607. The architect of his new house, built between 1607 and 1612, is not known: it may have been Newton himself, or he may have employed John Thorpe. Over the years some restoration and alterations took place and then, in 1877, an extension was built, to the designs of Norman Shaw, for the Maryon-Wilson family, who owned the house between 1767 and

1923. In 1911 Charlton House was still owned and lived in by the Maryon-Wilson family. The family gave permission for members of the Kent Archaeological Society to look around this magnificent Jacobean house. The family moved away during the First World War and, in 1920, the contents were sold. The house and park were bought by the Metropolitan Borough of Greenwich in 1925. The photograph on the left, taken on a warm summer's day, is a very good record of the exterior of the house before the north wing (in the foreground) was severely damaged in the Second World War. This wing was carefully restored after the war.

CHARLTON HOUSE TODAY, one of the finest surviving Jacobean houses, is a very popular community centre and library. From 1925 the house was used as a library, museum and council offices. During the Second World War, parts of the house were used for the Holidays at Home scheme and from this developed the idea of using it as a community centre. The museum collections, originally at Charlton House, are now at the Greenwich Heritage Centre.

NEW CHARLTON
AND
CHARLTON VALE

A VIEW FROM above Cox's Mount, Maryon Park, over New Charlton
in about 1900. Houses line Woolwich Road immediately below
the park. To the right of the chalk mound is Maryon Park School,
towering above the old houses of Charlton Vale. The school, opened
in 1896, is now Holborn College, but was previously known as
Woolwich College of Further Education. The 'hairpin' road is
Hardens Manorway, leading from Woolwich Road to the Thames.
At the bend in the road is the intriguingly named Lads of the Village
public house. This pub later changed its name, when London's great
flood barrier was built close by, to the Thames Barrier Tavern. It
closed in 1997 and became a veterinary surgery. The large factory
alongside the river to the right of Hardens Manorway is Siemens Bros

Telegraph Works. Behind the factory can be faintly seen the three masts of the Marine Society's training ship *Warspite*, moored near Charlton Pier.

A PLANE OR balloon would be needed to replicate this view today and attempts to take photographs from the top of the mount are hindered by the trees and foliage that make this part of Maryon Park so lovely. However, Chris Harrison's excellent photograph does clearly show some of the dramatic changes to the New Charlton landscape. There are light industrial units in the foreground, the Thames snaking its way down to the Thames barrier and Woolwich; further away, the landscape is dominated by the tall blocks of Canary Wharf and the huge and spectacular O_2 Arena on the Greenwich Peninsula.

KIDBROOKE LANE

KIDBROOKE LANE, WHICH linked the old village of Kidbrooke with Greenwich and Eltham, lost its rural aspect after the end of the Second World War when the London County Council covered the remaining farm fields with a series of housing estates. Brook Lane, the surviving remnant of Kidbrooke Lane, was incorporated into a small estate. The village green, an attractive rural feature, stood by Kidbrooke Lane and survived the building boom of the 1930s. However, a large portion of the green disappeared when the Rochester Way Relief Road was built across it in 1988. The parish church of St James in Kidbrooke Park Road was built in 1867. Close to the farm buildings in the photograph, a little further down the hill but out of view, was the site of the

medieval church of St Nicholas, later called St Blaise, which became derelict in the fifteenth century following the decline of the village. Modern flats stand on the site today. The photograph below was taken by A.R. Martin in 1938.

A RECENT VIEW from a similar viewpoint in Brook Lane. The present parish church of St James in Kidbrooke Park Road was badly damaged in the Second World War and restored in 1955 by Thomas Ford, but the spire was not replaced. A medical centre now stands on the site of the farm buildings.

KIDBROOKE'S FIELDS

THE PHOTOGRAPH ON the right was taken by A.R. Martin in the late 1930s and shows the fields of Kidbrooke just before they disappeared as a result of rapid suburban development. The new houses in Broad Walk can be seen on the right-hand side. Martin's family lived in Kidbrooke Park Road so he viewed the destruction of rural Kidbrooke with great sadness. He took many photographs prior to and during development: a unique record.

THE MODERN PICTURE above was taken from a similar viewpoint and shows how some of the old fields have survived as playing fields. There are fine views of London from this high point in Greenwich Cemetery: landmarks such as the Shard, the Gherkin, and the tall buildings in the City of London and Canary Wharf can be clearly seen.

ROYAL HERBERT HOSPITAL

THE ROYAL HERBERT Hospital was built as a hospital for Woolwich garrison in 1865 to replace an earlier hospital on Woolwich Common. This photo just shows the administration block of a huge complex. The architect was Sir Douglas Galton, a nephew of Florence Nightingale. It was named after Sir Sidney Herbert, who was War Minister when Florence was nursing during the Crimean War. No doubt she acted as an unpaid advisor during the building of the hospital. The writer Enid Bagnold, daughter of Colonel Bagnold, worked as a VAD (Voluntary Aid Detachment) nurse in the Royal Herbert during the First World War and later wrote the book *Diary Without Dates*, which revealed the 'them and us' treatment of wounded soldiers. On an adjacent site to the west of the Royal Herbert Hospital was the Brook Hospital – which had been, in the First World War, the Brook War Hospital. Built in 1896 as the South London Fever Hospital, Brook War Hospital was used in both world wars as an overspill military hospital. Queen Mary visited its wards in 1918. It served as a general hospital until it closed in 1995. The site was re-developed for housing but some of the original buildings were retained.

THE ROYAL HERBERT Hospital closed in 1978 when its replacement, the Queen Elizabeth Military Hospital, was built on Woolwich Common. The large hospital blocks were converted into housing units in the 1990s by Westcombe Homes. The Queen Elizabeth Military Hospital closed in 1995 but became a National Health Service hospital.

WOOLWICH FREE FERRY

THE *GORDON*, ONE of the original ferry boats, photographed in about 1907 (below). The Woolwich Free Ferry was opened on the 23 March 1889. The streets near the ferry terminal were decorated and there were celebrations as passengers, animals and carts were able to cross from South Woolwich to North Woolwich without paying a fare. This boat was named after General Gordon, who was born in Woolwich. New diesel boats replaced all the steamers in 1963, and in 1966 new terminals were opened.

THE *JOHN BURNS*, flagship of the ferry fleet, leaving the south ferry terminal heavily laden with lorries and cars (above). This boat is named after John Elliot Burns, who led the great dock strike of 1889 and later became a cabinet minister. The other boats in the small fleet are the *Ernest Bevin* and the *James Newman*. The North Woolwich landscape was dominated by the Royal Docks during the heyday of the old ferries, and now by large satellite dishes and planes taking off and landing at London City Airport, based in the former Royal Albert and King George V docks.

WOOLWICH ROYAL NAVAL DOCKYARD

THE MAIN GATES to the Royal Naval Dockyard in Woolwich Church Street. Henry VIII founded dockyards on either side of his palace at Greenwich in 1512-13: one at Woolwich and the other at Deptford. The original site of Woolwich dockyard – where his flagship, the *Henri Grace à Dieu*, was built in 1513 – was further east (next to the site of the Waterfront Leisure Centre) but by the 1530s it had moved westward. Here it grew substantially and became a huge complex with, in the nineteenth and twentieth centuries, its own railway system. Many fine fighting ships were built here. By the time of its closure by William Gladstone's administration it stretched from Mast Pond Wharf to Warspite Road. After its closure much of the site was acquired by the Royal Arsenal for military stores. Later, parts of the dockyard were sold and, in 1969, a large portion was bought by Greenwich Council for housing.

DOCKYARD GATES. WOOLWICH.

Molyneux Bro
35 William S
Woolwich.

IN THE MODERN view on the right the main gate is less ornate but little changed. It is now the entrance to a housing estate. The late eighteenth-century Clockhouse, originally the dockyard's offices, is now a community centre, and the eighteenth-century gatehouse, which was for a while the Gatehouse public house, has been converted into housing. Two dry docks and a gun bastion have also been preserved.

In 1980 a 'riverside promenade' was laid along the length of the estate. By walking east to west along this riverside walk, the amazing Thames Barrier is clearly visible. This barrier was built by the Greater London Council between 1974 and 1982 and, as a piece of engineering, is on a par with many great nineteenth-century projects and is admired throughout the world. The stainless steel hoods are a prominent feature. Ships and other river craft are able to pass through the four gaps in the central piers because the massive gates rest on the river bed. The barrier runs between New Charlton on the south bank, where there is a visitor centre, and Thames Barrier Park in Silvertown on the north. When the gates are closed the Thames to the west becomes a large lake. In 2007 the gates were closed twice because of a storm surge in the North Sea. The barrier will continue to protect London from flooding for many decades to come.

WELLINGTON STREET, WOOLWICH

WELLINGTON STREET FORMS part of the main
road from Charlton. The photograph on the right
was taken from the northern end of the street where
it became Greens End. In 1900 the newly formed
Metropolitan Borough of Woolwich decided to build
an impressive new Town Hall in Wellington Street.
It was designed by the architect Sir Alfred Brumwell
Thomas in 'High Edwardian Baroque' style. Its tall
clock tower dominated the area. The main entrance
leads into the Victoria Hall where there is a statue of
Queen Victoria. Another feature of the building is the
many stained glass windows illustrating historical

figures and events linked with Woolwich. The Town Hall was finished in 1906. Adjacent to the Town Hall is the very capacious Grand Theatre, built in 1899/1900. The theatre had become a cinema by 1923 and was demolished in 1939 when a purpose-built cinema took its place. The cinema was converted into a nightclub – which was itself closed in 2008. However, the building is soon to re-open as Woolwich Grand Theatre!

THERE HAVE BEEN remarkable changes to Wellington Street with the completion in 2011 of Greenwich Council's fine new office buildings and library. They stand opposite Sir Alfred Brumwell Thomas' splendid Town Hall. The new buildings include a spacious, modern library to replace the original building in Calderwood Street. Below the Town Hall are buildings that have variously been Woolwich Polytechnic, Thames Polytechnic, University of Greenwich and now Anglian College. Elliston House, a tower block, rises in the background behind the Town Hall.

POWIS STREET, WOOLWICH

THIS STREET WAS laid out in 1782, and building began in around 1798. It is named after the Powis family who owned a successful brewery in Greenwich. They also owned land in Woolwich. At the end of the nineteenth century Powis Street was redesigned and became known for its collection of fashionable stores such as Cuffs, Garrets, Furlong's Furniture Stores and the head office of the Royal Arsenal Co-operative Society. The Furlong family started to make furniture in Woolwich in 1812. They also became estate agents, auctioneers and undertakers. On busy

POWIS STREET, WOOLWICH

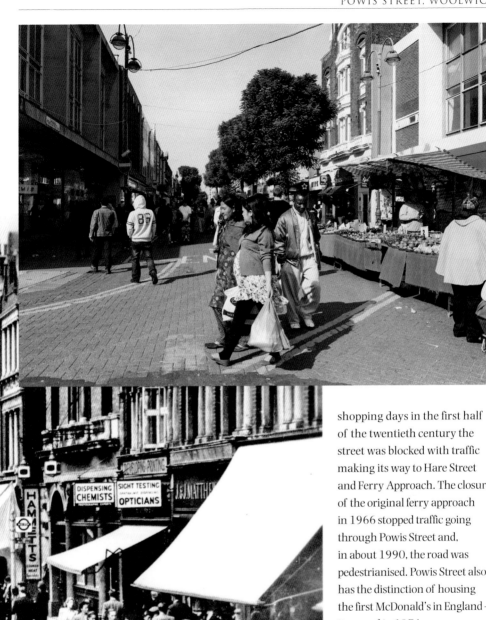

shopping days in the first half of the twentieth century the street was blocked with traffic making its way to Hare Street and Ferry Approach. The closure of the original ferry approach in 1966 stopped traffic going through Powis Street and, in about 1990, the road was pedestrianised. Powis Street also has the distinction of housing the first McDonald's in England – it opened in 1974.

POWIS STREET IS still Woolwich's main shopping street as it has been throughout the nineteenth and twentieth centuries; it is always busy, even though the department stores have all gone.

71

ROYAL ARSENAL CO-OP
SOCIETY'S GENERAL STORE

IN 1868 SOME Royal Arsenal workers started the Royal Arsenal Supply Association. They traded from small private houses in Woolwich until 1873 when, having changed the name to the Royal Arsenal Co-operative Society, their first shop was opened in Powis Street. Early members of the society referred to it as 'The Stores'. The RACS grew rapidly, and as well as opening many more shops it built low-cost housing, purchased a farm on the slopes of Shooters Hill and bought a large house called Shornells as an educational centre. The large central store in Powis Street was built in 1903, which is when the photograph opposite was taken. A statue of Alexander McLeod, a founder of the RACS, was placed in the entrance hall. In 1938 a new large store was opened in Powis Street. This new Co-op shop was opposite the 1903 building with its splendid clock tower. The new art-deco style was in complete contrast to the earlier building with its tall windows and splendid tower. The old photograph of Powis Street captured the tower at the west end of the street. In 1985 the RACS merged with the Co-operative Wholesale Society and the 1938 building was used as the CWS regional office.

Nos 125-161 POWIS Street, the former head offices of the Royal Arsenal Co-operative Society, with scaffolding obscuring its fine dome, can be seen in the modern photograph below. It seems that Greenwich Council will soon vacate this building and that there is a proposal to use it as a budget hotel.

HARE STREET, WOOLWICH

THE PHOTOGRAPH BELOW was taken in about 1905. Hare Street had been rebuilt at the beginning of the twentieth century and, with shops like Lipton's tea and provisions merchants

and Leavey's outfitters and drapers, it was a popular shopping street. From 1889 to the 1960s, Hare Street was one of the main routes to the Free Ferry and thus very congested.

HARE STREET NO longer leads to Ferry Approach and the Free Ferry, so is fairly free of traffic. At the end of the street can just be seen the entrance to the Waterfront Leisure Centre, built over the site of the old approach to the Free Ferry.

WOOLWICH ARSENAL STATION AND WOOLWICH NEW ROAD

CABBIES WAIT OUTSIDE the 1905 entrance to the station in the wonderful old photograph on the right. The station was originally opened in 1849 with an entrance in Vincent Road. The building on the extreme right of the photograph was once the Duke of Connaught's Coffee Tavern. The proprietor introduced the 'Arsenal Breakfast' after an eight-hour day was introduced at the Royal Arsenal in 1894. Between the hours of 7.00 a.m. and 10.00 p.m. the food was served from counters on either side of the main entrance. In 1906 food gave way to travel when Thomas Cook and Son took over the corner snack bar and converted it into a travel office. Cook's Tours eventually moved to Powis Street. At the end of the Second World War the basement of the old building was used as a jazz club. The George

Webb Dixielanders recruited a young trumpet player named Humphrey Lyttleton, who later started his own band. Many famous jazz performers played in Woolwich in the 1940s and 1950s.

WOOLWICH NEW ROAD still has some interesting old buildings but the street is now dominated by two important station buildings. Woolwich Arsenal rail station, a high-tech building of 1993, was built on the site of an earlier station. Adjoining it on the far side is the Woolwich terminus of the Docklands Light Railway, which opened in 2009. Woolwich's transport links will be further enhanced when the Crossrail station opens in the future, giving direct access to central London and Heathrow Airport.

WOOLWICH MARKET

THE CHARTER FOR Woolwich market dates from 1619, and the market was first held on Market Hill, close to the Thames. In 1888 it moved to Beresford Square. The 1923 photograph on the right features the High Pavement, which was well known for its fruit stalls. After 1888, shops opened around Beresford Square, and shops such as Birt's jewellers shop, Mence Smith's hardware store and Pickford's, travel agents and removers, were on the High Pavement. Before 1939, Beresford Square was also used for political meetings, a source of free entertainment with hecklers having a heyday.

WOOLWICH MARKET STILL flourishes, selling a wide variety of products, although the High Pavement was closed for refurbishment when the modern photograph on the left was taken. The Beresford Gate is prominent in the background of both photographs.

THE BERESFORD GATE, ROYAL ARSENAL

THE BERESFORD GATE was built in three stages: 1829, 1859 and 1891. It was the main gate into the Royal Arsenal. The Royal Arsenal Ordnance factory was the main employer in Woolwich for nearly 300 years. Established at the end of the seventeenth century, buildings and testing grounds gradually spread eastwards until some three miles of Plumstead Marshes were enclosed. The Royal Arsenal had its own railway systems and piers and wharves on the riverside. In the photograph on the right (taken in around 1914), a tram to Abbey Wood stops to pick up workers, many of whom lived on the Bostall Estate, which was built by the Royal Arsenal Co-operative Society. Over 70,000 people, including many women, worked in the Royal Arsenal in the First World War. The Arsenal survived the Second World War, although it was bombed during the Blitz. Holy Trinity church, built in 1852, is opposite the cinema (which is advertising continuous performances

BERESFORD SQUARE

between 3.00 p.m. and 10.00 p.m.). In the 1960s this area was changed. The cinema and Holy Trinity church were demolished and the ordnance factories suffered cuts in work and staff. The Royal Ordnance factories closed in 1967, but the Ministry of Defence didn't finally leave the site until 1994. In 1986, a new dual carriageway was built between the Beresford Gate and the Royal Arsenal.

THE BERESFORD GATE, detached from the Arsenal, is now a very prominent feature of Beresford Square and the market has spread right up to it. Before 1986 the narrow and congested main road ran between the square and the gate. Holy Trinity church, which stood at the junction of Beresford Street and Rope Yard Rails, was closed in 1960 and demolished two years later. In the modern photograph the only building to be seen beyond the gate is a small public convenience.

ROYAL ARTILLERY BARRACKS, WOOLWICH COMMON

THE 1912 PHOTOGRAPH on the right features the Royal Artillery barracks on Woolwich Common. The Royal Regiment of Artillery was founded in 1716 in Woolwich Warren (later renamed the Royal Arsenal). It was difficult to expand the barracks on that site, so land was acquired adjacent to Woolwich Common and an imposing building, reminiscent of the Winter Palace in St Petersburg, was built between 1778 and 1802, and described as 'the longest architectural

composition in London'. Between 1802 and 1806 the Board of Ordnance bought Woolwich Common. With the building of the Royal Military Academy on the common, the whole area was given over to army use. At the end of the path in the photograph are official notices, such as 'the Barrack Field is closed to the public, by order'.

THE ROYAL ARTILLERY moved from Woolwich to Larkhill in 2007. The barracks now house companies of Grenadier Guards and Coldstream Guards; The 2nd Battalion, The Princess of Wales's Royal Regiment and the King's Troop Royal Horse Artillery. Refurbishment is taking place in time for the Olympic and Paralympic shooting events in 2012. Opposite the barracks in Grand Depot Road is the ruined Royal Garrison church of St George, built by Thomas Wyatt in 1863. Darrell Spurgeon, a writer of fine local guidebooks, refers to it as 'a striking and impressive ruin'. It was bombed in 1944 but is preserved as a memorial garden. The chapel interior is soon to be restored and a new fabric roof will be constructed to protect the interior with its memorials from the elements. The chapel will then be open to the public. This view of the barracks is framed by the west door of the Garrison church.

WOOLWICH COMMON

IN 1968 THE façades of these buildings overlooked the Garrison Sport Ground. The group of buildings ran from Nightingale Place along the edge of the common and included some fine terraces, notably Kempt Terrace (where General Charles Gordon was born in 1833), as well as the late eighteenth-century Barrack Tavern. The houses in the panorama, once the abode of army officers and military cramming schools, were gradually converted into flats and shops. In the 1920s, Gordon's house, No. 29 Woolwich Common, became a hostel for the Young Women's

Christian Association. In 1964 the London County Council and the Ministry of Housing and Local Government refused to allow demolition of these eighteenth- and nineteenth-century buildings. The Woolwich Common Redevelopment Area Plan of 1969-70 disregarded the recommendations. In the teeth of great opposition, particularly from the Woolwich and District Antiquarian Society, this fine group was demolished in 1972 to make way for the western edge of the Woolwich Common estate.

THE FRONTAGE OF the Woolwich Common estate was described by Darrell Spurgeon as 'jagged, restless and tiered'. The obelisk memorial to Robert John Little, a marine who died in 1861, and part of Government House on the corner of Nightingale Place can just be glimpsed. The Woolwich Common estate was built between 1967 and 1982.

PLUMSTEAD HIGH STREET

THE YEAR IS 1882 and the men clustered around the lamp post outside the Green Man public house look as though they are waiting for a posse to ride into town. Not so – just a scene in the High Street on the brink of change. The men could be builders: there is scaffolding at the Green Man and maybe the pub is about to be rebuilt. Certainly, within a few years, both the Green Man and the Red Lion were rebuilt. Possibly the photographer is aware that the old village street is going to be drastically altered with the building of many new streets to house the huge labour force at the Royal Arsenal in neighbouring Woolwich. The barrel and table in the gutter

belong to the greengrocer standing outside his shop. The grocer at No. 79 advertises a 'Tea Mart' on his lamp. Beyond the Red Lion public house sign are buildings on the corner of Cage Lane, later renamed Lakedale Road. The women, deep in conversation, seem to be unaware of the photographer.

THE GREEN MAN public house was rebuilt after the original photograph was taken. Now it trades as O'Dowd's. Further up the street, at No. 95. is the Red Lion, now a noodle bar. Plumstead High Street is part of an ancient way that linked many riverside communities, including Woolwich and Greenwich. Roman remains have been found along its route, an indication of its antiquity.

PLUMSTEAD LIBRARY

PLUMSTEAD LIBRARY WAS opened in 1904 after a successful campaign called 'Why Plumstead Needs a Library'. A red brick building with bowed windows on either side of the entrance, the exterior is like a very large and comfortable house! The posters alongside the library advertise 'Westward Ho, the popular smoking mixture' and a Bank-Holiday fête and gala at Repository Grounds, Woolwich. The people in the 1905 photograph on the right look relaxed and cheerful. Across the adjacent side street were Plumstead Baths, also built at the beginning of the twentieth century. There was an overall plan to have maximum use of the baths by making it possible to turn a large pool into a hall – a temporary measure to give people a

decent local dance hall. Plumstead Baths held 'Jolly Dances' every Saturday night. The price was 6*d* for dancing and 3*d* to sit in the balcony. Learners could buy an hour's tuition for 6*d*. A fancy-dress carnival in January 1911 was run by Mr Bloodworth. The local press reported that 'Bloodworth's Jolly Dances were an absolute success'. The baths have been demolished.

THE EXTERIOR OF Plumstead Library has changed little since its opening in 1904 but there have been many changes inside. An important early change was the opening of the Borough Museum on the first floor in 1919. The museum's important collections of local history, archaeology and natural history were transferred in 2003 to the Greenwich Heritage Centre in the Royal Arsenal when the borough's Local History Library and Museum Service merged.

ST JOHN'S CHURCH, ELTHAM

ST JOHN'S PARISH church, pictured in 1895. The church was built in 1875 on a site where there had been a church from about 1115. Designed by Sir Arthur Blomfield, this parish church was an integral part of Eltham High Street until 1905, when Well Hall Road was extended to form a crossroads by St John's. Whitworth House, to the right of the church, was demolished to make way for the road. The two buildings seen beyond the church were the vicarage and Eltham Brewery. Buried in the churchyard are Thomas Doggett (died 1721), the founder of Doggett's Coat and Badge race which is held on the Thames every year, and Yemmerrawanyea Kebbarah, who died in 1794. Kebbarah was one of two Australian Aborigines to visit Europe in the era.

THE MODERN PHOTOGRAPH above shows the busy junction of Eltham High Street, Court Road and Well Hall Road: so different to the peaceful scene of the 1890s before Well Hall Road had been made. The vicarage and the brewery, significant landmarks, have long since been demolished.

ELTHAM HIGH STREET

BY 1933 ELTHAM High Street had been widened and some old buildings demolished.
However, the Greyhound public house and Mellin's the Chemist are still there. The prominent

HIGH STREET, ELTHAM.

dome of the Palace Cinema is further up the High Street. The Congregational church on the corner of the High Street and Well Hall Road was closed in 1935 and demolished. A McDonald's is now on the site.

THE YELLOW LINES of the box junction distract the eye a little from the village survivals in the high street: the Olde Greyhound, rebuilt in 1978 but retaining its 1720s style, and Mellin's Wine Bar buildings, which also dates from the same era. These old buildings are precious parts of the streetscape.

THE TUDOR BARN, ELTHAM

IN THE EARLY sixteenth century, William Roper acquired the estate of Well Hall. He was married to Margaret, daughter of Sir Thomas More, and his estate in Eltham was close to Eltham Palace (which had become Crown property in 1305 and soon became a major Plantaganet palace). The Great Hall of Eltham Palace was built in around 1480, and Henry VIII, who spent his childhood there, made further improvements. During Henry's reign Greenwich Palace took precedence and Eltham Palace appears to have been used as a grand hunting lodge and a venue

for state business. The Lord Chancellor's Lodgings in the courtyard were used by Sir Thomas More and William Roper was attached to More's staff. More was executed for high treason in 1535. The Roper mansion at Well Hall was built on the site of a previous house within a moat. In the eighteenth century the mansion was demolished but the fine domestic outbuildings were saved. When the 1911 photograph on the left was taken, the site was known as Well Hall Farm. In 1930 Woolwich Borough Council bought the buildings and renamed them the Tudor Barn.

THE SIXTEENTH-CENTURY buildings have not changed externally a great deal but the present Tudor Barn Restaurant is a world away from the farmyard setting of the original picture. It is quite a story: built as a modern extension to the medieval manor house in the sixteenth century, it later became a farm building, then a restaurant and art gallery run by the local authority and finally a smart eating place in beautifully restored grounds.

Other titles published by The History Press

Maritime Greenwich
DAVID RAZMAN

For over a thousand years Greenwich was the site of a thriving ship and boatbuilding industry. A variety of ships were built up and down the Thames, and the riverfront itself was filled with cranes, wharfages and ships loading or un-loading their cargoes. A multitude of river craft, from small rowboats to giant steamers, once made their way along this point in the river, and the boroughs of Greenwich, Deptford and Woolwich became synonymous with new technology and engineering.

978 0 7524 4778 0

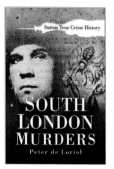

South London Murders
PETER DE LORIOL

Over the centuries South London has witnessed literally thousands of murders: those included within the pages of this book have shocked, fascinated and enthralled the public and commentators for generations. Some of these cases were milestones in the annals of crime detection such as those in which fingerprinting and DNA testing were used for the first time. In this fascinating book, well-remembered crimes are featured alongside those that have been forgotten for centuries.

978 0 7509 4426 7

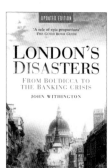

London's Disasters: from Boudicca to the Banking Crisis
JOHN WITHINGTON

London has been hit by wave upon wave of destruction, and this fascinating and unique book tells the story of over 2000 years of disaster from fire, water, disease, pollution, accident, storm, riot, terrorism and enemy action. It chronicles well-known episodes like the Great Plague of 1655 and the Blitz, as well as lesser-known events such as whirlwinds and earthquakes. London's Disasters ultimately celebrates the spirit of its people who have risen above it all and for whom London is one of the greatest cities on earth.

978 0 7524 5747 5

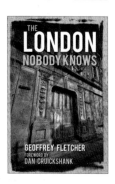

The London Nobody Knows
GEOFFREY FLETCHER

Geoffrey Fletcher's off-beat portrayal of London does not focus on the big landmarks but rather 'the tawdry, extravagant and eccentric'. His descriptions will transport you to an art nouveau pub, a Victorian music hall, a Hawksmoor church and even a public toilet in Holborn in which the attendant kept goldfish in the cisterns. Drawn to the corners where 'the kids swarm like ants and there are dogs everywhere', Fletcher will take you to parts of the city where few outsiders venture.

978 0 7524 6199 1

Visit our website and discover thousands of other History Press books.
www.thehistorypress.co.uk

The History Press